Planting Seeds

Written by Katherine Chu

GRL Consultant, Diane Craig, Certified Literacy Specialist

I0869377

Pull Ahead READERS

Lerner Publications ◆ Minneapolis

Note from a GRL Consultant
This Pull Ahead leveled book has been carefully designed for beginning readers. A team of guided reading literacy experts has reviewed and leveled the book to ensure readers pull ahead and experience success.

Lerner Publications
An imprint of Lerner Publishing Group, Inc.
241 First Avenue North
Minneapolis, MN 55401 USA

For reading levels and more information, look up this title at www.lernerbooks.com.

Main body text set in Memphis Pro 24/39
Typeface provided by Linotype.

Photo Acknowledgments
The images in this book are used with the permission of: © ArtCookStudio/Adobe Stock, p. 3; © Gregory Johnston/Shutterstock Images, pp. 4–5; © HTWE/Shutterstock Images, pp. 6–7, 16 (right); © lovelyday12/Shutterstock Images, pp. 8–9; © rodimovpavel/Adobe Stock, pp. 10–11; © MEE KO DONG/Shutterstock Images, pp. 12–13, 16 (middle); © cycreation/Adobe Stock, pp. 14–15, 16 (left).

Front cover: © Floki/Adobe Stock

Library of Congress Cataloging-in-Publication Data

Names: Chu, Katherine, author.
Title: Planting seeds / written by Katherine Chu.
Description: Minneapolis : Lerner Publications , [2025] | Series: In the garden (pull ahead readers - nonfiction) | Includes index. | Audience: Ages 4–7 | Audience: Grades K–1 | Summary: "Plant your seeds, water the soil, and watch your garden grow! This engaging and carefully leveled text teaches emergent readers about growing a garden with seeds. Pairs with the fiction title Sidney's Seeds"—Provided by publisher.
Identifiers: LCCN 2024009151 (print) | LCCN 2024009152 (ebook) | ISBN 9798765647776 (lib. bdg.) | ISBN 9798765661949 (paperback) | ISBN 9798765655511 (epub)
Subjects: LCSH: Seeds—Juvenile literature. | Planting (Plant culture)—Juvenile literature.
Classification: LCC SB117 .C483 2025 (print) | LCC SB117 (ebook) | DDC 631.5/21—dc23/eng/20240423

LC record available at https://lccn.loc.gov/2024009151
LC ebook record available at https://lccn.loc.gov/2024009152

Manufactured in the United States of America
1 – CG – 12/15/24

Table of Contents

Planting Seeds

Seeds come in different shapes and sizes.

Seeds need soil, water, and sunlight.

I can dig holes in the soil. I can put seeds in the holes.

Then I can water the seeds.

Then I watch the seeds turn into plants.

I can grow a garden with seeds!

Did You See It?

garden

plant

soil

Index